W0017895

THE HARVEST
&
THE LAMP

COLOSSEUM BOOKS

JAMES MATTHEW WILSON, SERIES EDITOR

THE HARVEST
&
THE LAMP

POEMS BY

ANDREW FRISARDI

FRANCISCAN UNIVERSITY PRESS

Copyright © 2020 by Franciscan University Press
All rights reserved.
No part of this publication may be reproduced or transmitted in any form or means,
electronic or mechanical, including photography, recording, or any other information
storage or retrieval system, without permission in writing from the publisher. Requests
for permission to make copies of any part of the work should be directed to:

Franciscan University Press
1235 University Boulevard
Steubenville, OH 43952
740-283-3771

Distributed by:
The Catholic University of America Press
c/o HFS
P.O. Box 50370
Baltimore, MD 21211
800-537-5487

Library of Congress Cataloging-in-Publication Data
Names: Frisardi, Andrew, author.
Title: The harvest and the lamp / poems by Andrew Frisardi.
Description: Steubenville, OH : Franciscan University Press, [2020] | Series: Colosseum
books ; 3 | Summary: "The Harvest and the Lamp, the third volume of the Colosseum Books
series, is a singular collection of poems in an wide variety of forms and voices. Author
Andrew Frisardi writes on fundamental human themes such as love and desire, death and
grief, the nature of the self and self-transcendence in a tone that ranges from serious to witty
to exuberant. The poems are often set in Italy, where Frisardi has lived for a number of
years, drawing on natural or concrete imagery as well as the imaginal or symbolic. Frisardi
composes in a number of forms: sonnet and sestina, triolet and ghazal, nonce forms and
free verse, gracefully and with a fresh use of diction and rhyme. As the late poet-translator
Brett Foster put it, 'Andrew Frisardi's [poems] are exquisitely made things, many angled
and shining brightly. Ear, eye, and mind do their elegant, exact work.' Frisardi is an
internationally noted translator and independent scholar of Dante, and Dante's impact
appears directly or indirectly in much of his poetry, including a few translations in this
volume. The poet-biographer Paul Mariani has written that in Frisardi's poetry one finds the
'resins of the classics everywhere. Add wit, sensitivity, humor and the recurring shock
of recognition, then sit back and enjoy what Andrew Frisardi has prepared for you. Then
come back and taste again for the sheer pleasure of the company.'" — Provided by publisher.
Identifiers: LCCN 2020027931 | ISBN 9781733988964 (paperback)
Subjects: LCGFT: Poetry.
Classification: LCC PS3606.R5738 H37 2020 | DDC 811/.6 — dc23
LC record available at https://lccn.loc.gov/2020027931

Text and cover design by Kachergis Book Design
Cover and title pages lettering: Gaynor Goffe
Printed in the United States of America.

The translation on p. 38, *You pilgrims walking by, oblivious,* is reprinted
(with minor emendations) courtesy of Northwestern University Press (Evanston,
Illinois), from Dante Alighieri, *Vita nova.* English translation, introduction,
and notes copyright © 2012 by Andrew Frisardi.
Published 2012 by Northwestern University Press.
All rights reserved.

FOR DAPHNE

CONTENTS

I

SPRING INTO NIGHT

Because I could not stop for Death —
He kindly stopped for me.

EMILY DICKINSON

The Yellow Moth

I.M. PETER RUSSELL

Orvieto, floating on its cliff in mist,
Seems Avalonish now: the Duomo's spires
Distinct but its facade's gold glimmer hidden.
As I walk home a sudden spray of rain
Covers my face, a fecund dung-tinged wind
Arriving from the land of infidels.
A rooster flashes his fancy tail feather
Beside groomed vineyards, and the fields are dressed
In brown corduroy. Clouds break loose, drifting
Westward, and the sun touches twigs and muck,
The first pale green and a cow's bony back.

And here a yellow moth flutters
In my trajectory, abrupt, like Psyche.
Psyche who never flies direct.
Psyche who is as light as thought
But a lot more susceptible to wind.

The yellow flicker holds a hint of green:
The resurrection-yellow of mimosa.
How does the earth do it, year after year
Becoming young again? In sodden grass
The lambs are gamboling their lives away.

Where I am in the world it's Lent, *Quaresima*.
Grotesques of Carnival that celebrate

Flesh have given way to vigils and ash.
And yet this ancient custom happens right
When spring is set, as if to say rebirth
Is not a given, it's what we create
By art amid the accidents of fate,
And in our times of dying — call it grace.

The yellow moth flits this way now, now that,
Its sweet and bitter yellow watering
My wordless tongue. Hello, mimosa moth:
Mystery that is the world's least hidden thing.

Easter Morning

PRIME

At dawn, the shapes of cypresses in fog
Were fingers pointing up from graves, as if what's born
Might rouse the dead into an epilogue
Of mist that lifted, leaving swatches in whitethorn.

TERCE

My breath's the ectoplasm of a ghost
In ringing air. The local churches call
The faithful while I mark the creed of lost
Beginnings on the switchback up the hill.

The farmland outside Rocca Ripesena
Is a winding-sheet about to open.
The uncut grasses, curled and white with rain,
Are loosening to face the sun upslope.

From a bush nearby I hear an unknown whistle,
Indomitably upbeat: "Wake! It's time!"
The birds are in their skeletal cathedral
And I am in my body that's not mine.

I see a finch perched on a branch's suture,
Hopping into the darkness of the future.

Roll Call at Acheron

The sound was coming from so far away
We thought at first it was the breath we missed
The moment we were dead, that very day.

It neared us like a moan inside a mist
Of wishes, harmonizing with the hum
Of silence from a newly pulseless wrist.

It was the sigh that light gives when the sum
Of zeroes grazes hills, cicadas saw
The day in half, and working men succumb.

We all were at the river of our raw
Awakening, awaiting each to board
In turn to cross the current of a thaw.

Some balked at the sound, frightened. Some adored
Its strange articulations as it came
Like feathers, hovering. Some murmured, *Lord.*

The sound each heard as either grace or blame
Was wind that called us: name by name by name.

The Casket and the Crib

The organ bank had come to claim her debt.
They'd pierced her flesh like soldiers at the Cross,
And divvied up her parts, and placed a bet
On what they'd use, and written off their loss.
Now I was left like someone on the take
At what would be a proper Irish wake.

"It's sad," she'd told me only weeks before,
"To slight the body like it's in the grave
Already. It's a friend, and friends count more
The more they're irreplaceable." She gave
The world to me in childhood, and its yield
Was all of what I leaned on where I kneeled.

The line of viewers gabbed, as she'd prefer,
Though no one could outtalk her silence. I
Could only watch her face that wasn't her,
Although the undertaker's art did try
To mask the repossession. Memory lingers,
A rosary winding in and out her fingers.

I wept — like any raw, extracted rib.
I was an infant now, *she* gazing down
At *me*, the casket suddenly a crib
I was inside, held by her eyes' soft brown.
With her now dead and me again just born,
I started living where she had been torn.

Remembering Sunflowers

As if to call love back, when fields of flowers had bent
Once more to face the twilight, the early sun returned.
His mother's voice and scent is where his memory went,
As if to call love back, when fields of flowers had bent
Their burning heads in circles towards the orient
Of fire and ash. His very learning he unlearned,
As if to call love back when fields of flowers had bent.
Once more, to face the twilight, the early son returned.

For That Which Has Fallen

ALL SAINTS

For that which has fallen,
Moisture-seeking crawlers
And palsied hands of leaves
Unclasp summer's trophies.
For that which has fallen,
The moon's a beggar's bowl.
For that which has fallen
Come those who've passed over
Beyond the veil of sight
On hieroglyphic feathers
Inscrutable forever,
With light, air, and mist
Tangled gray in branches,
With ghouls that guard our doors,
With olives and horse-chestnuts
In silver dreams and armor —
For that which has fallen
Returns. And as for us,
We wish, we come to see,
To go down, tired or happy,
To that which has fallen.

The Apricot Tree

This year, I think, we will have apricots.
The tree down at the bottom of the garden,
Which seemed a splintered twist of bark that rots
Within, is blossoming February's pardon.
Last year the fruit it gave us was negated:
Shaded light that cooled the afternoon
Like grief no one was ready yet to prune
The useless branches from. And so we waited.

Serena, oracle of cats, is staring
Past it, seated on the ragged slope,
As if she might divine how things are faring
Where we can't see. Her stillness ripens hope
That what's still possible will soon appear,
Like apricots I think we'll have this year.

Snowfall in Lent

Mimosa came unsought
In sunbursts on my hill.
Then snow hid, dot by dot,
My straightedge windowsill,

Which, like a guillotine,
Had severed out from in.
Now that the cut is clean,
Compunction, pull the pin.

Stream

AFTER READING RICHARD WILBUR'S
"HAMLEN BROOK"

Gliding upon cascades of sound,
The crumpled leaves that ride the rush
Make visible a crystal underhush
That gives the movement ground.

With wreckage that its current bears,
The stream is murmuring through a glen
Surrender to the eddying amen
Of stillness it declares.

Solitude

You've tried to nail a board
To waves, whisper an ode
To jackhammers, and goad
A gut to strum a chord.

You even tossed a string
Up to the sky at night
To try and catch a kite.

Now it is time to bring
Yourself back, yeast to flour;
Unfold a face you put
Once in a chest, your foot
Pressed flat against the hour.

If, added, one makes two,
Its quotient must be you.

No Photo

I.M. JOHN HAINES

1.

In an old photo of you bent
Over your traps and nets,
Your body's shape is darker
Even than the Alaska ridge
In the distance. You were almost
The age that I am now — by now,
A fiction that survives reality.

2.

To run and run and not look back
Is the fate of anyone who's born
Into a state of perpetual war.
Home has to be made from what's
At hand, to touch the world
You have to let it go.

3.

You seem the very face of snow,
The arms and legs of the wood
You stacked split on the porch.
Where do spring's profusions head
In winter? No photo I hold
Could trace them. You couldn't stay
Forever but the trees face north.

Nostalgia for the Future

Resolutions I am the last to fathom,
Though they're mine, including their blind perspective;
Stumbled-on decisions like afterthoughts which
Patterned my actions:

Place that looks out towards and beseeches memory:
There now, are you happy about what's happened,
Coming here to follow a river backwards,
Cutting the valley?

Something kept me where I had not intended.
Portents now seem rumors that superstition
Babbles as it goes, an unlikely story
Passed down the seasons.

Summer afternoons the cicadas sawing
Shadows, trunks of hopefulness falling, sundown
Flickering. All my ghosts can return in any
Form that disarms me.

Commute

1.

What did I expect
when I stepped out
into the drizzly morning
and handed coins
to the man at the corner?
The cars and *motorini*
jolted at the lights,
and the world and all its people
were there to remind me
of something — I'm still
not sure exactly what.

2.

I could just
step off the platform
to catch the train
before I miss it
again. That warm
passage is trust.

3.

All the commuters looking out
of windows at the hurtling world
uproot trees, break down
branches and boulders to debris,
even the daylight kindled

from the darkness that light is
without eyes. The world's
in blazes in our brains:
humus in fields,
shadows under ploughing,
litter of torn paper birds.

4.

The train stops in a field,
where a mare champing hay
watches us watching her.
Bits of straw ray from her lips,
the train reflected in her eyes.
We're looking at her looking.
The horse of solid earth,
keeper of perfect graves,
is seeing us.

5.

This could take a while,
just a matter of time.
We might wait suspended
until we feel the first slippage of wind
unsettling the tomb's lid.

First Signs of Spring

The lilies, as forecast, are baring their throats.

The sun in its unclouded moment
lights up raindrops on shoots
which shimmer, milky, viscous.

Walking into a barnyard,
suddenly
you realize you're strutting
like a rooster.

A gust
of water, crowd mentality
of the elements,
swipes your arms and face.

And now your elbows
are pumping at your sides,

a sound escapes
your tensile mouth
that resembles nothing
you've ever thought:

The king hath lain with the queen! you blurt.

And the hens scatter
like tiny tyrannosaurs.

A *Casalinga* in Spring

She is a needle in the haystack of her housecoat.
Lugging a bucket and a hand-stained stick,
She throws a white rag down in the corridors
Of *marmo finto*, then out on the flagstone walk,
Streaked with runoff. The west wind
From the foothills, winging in sheets,
Rushes the clothesline like a feathered bull,
A *Maremmano* fresh from grazing salt
Who is suddenly in love with lilies.

She is the handmaid of the lord,
Her husband, who calls her as she bends
To wring the hours from her hands.
Her curved back forms a question mark.

Her window curtains bloat like cherubs chanting
Ammonia alleluias, and her eyes
And nostrils flare against the scouring light.
It might be Easter but perhaps it's not.
The mop head that she pushes never dies.

The Last Sunday before the Cruelest Month

An O of sky proclaims *Cerulean*
Above the heathery hallelujah hills
And cypress-evergreens' air-tower controls,
A perfect landing pad in powder blue
For putti, but the gunmetal cloudbank
Girdling it glowers down and blackly says:

Till further notice the sensuous ya-yas
Of spring will be postponed.

                            The dogs don't dig it.
Their chains go *Drag drag drag* on ponderous lawns.
A baby yowls, while Time and Eternity loudly
Get it on again — they do that on Sundays.
And the remainder of the week is history.

Gibbous

The moon at times is hunched and old,
Deformed, a decadent yellow,
A jealous seed of sun gone cold,
A decrepit has-been fellow.

He's leering at the summer night,
Rising in a sea of sweat
Above the hill town's wavering light,
Tumid, heavy, pocked, and wet.

Rain at Night

The city lies back in its winding-sheet
While little digits drum a steady beat

On roofs and terraces, and rolling rain
Crescendos in the hushed collective brain.

Pensioner, wage-enslaved, impoverished, posh,
The sleeping people feel it wash wash wash

In runnels, through dark tunnels under grids
And manholes, down detritus till it rids

The buildup. Hands like these may be minute,
But such masseuses' touches work the root,

As buried wishes loosen from debris
And multitudes of deltas meet the sea.

II

AFTERLIFE
IN THE PROVINCES

For nothing can be sole or whole
That has not been rent.

W. B. YEATS

Aubades

When I woke up today, my lips
Smooshed against your shoulder,
Your face's outline was a blurred eclipse
Of yesterday, a light that had grown older.
My palm and fingers curved atop your breast
Like effigies at rest.

Our sleeping in the course of years
Has made our bodies fit
Together as a rippling current clears
In passing over depths that ballast it.
Your wedding dress was cloth we had to forage
With little left in storage,

In the home where we first lived together,
When we called off all bets
Of change for change. We didn't know yet whether
What we had in store would pay our debts,
While whooshes on the distant interstate
Sustained a constant rate,

And at the window-box we fed
The finches' great insistence,
As we were making plans to get ahead
Of where the future swallowed up the distance.
Unwitting cowbirds, ad-lib and uncouth,
We gave away our youth

As winter light began to leach
From the sky. The unemphatic
Sun was an ancient hand that couldn't reach
A lamp for being tired or rheumatic,
The mornings we caressed each other's skin
As we watched time begin.

Fall Moon

Another winter coming and I'm talking to myself.
I'm setting up my wine and oil on the cellar shelf
In demijohns and jars as relics of my lucky stars.
It's getting late. The more time flows the icier its scars.
I can't tell if I pass through seasons or they pass through me.
I'm pulpy as the ripened fruit on my persimmon tree,
Whose leaves have fallen. In the distance, Mount Soratte's cone
Is floating like an island where the tide of clouds has blown.
A raven grouches past defoliated pylon wire
Across the valley toward the setting sun's sputtering fire,
Which the moon, a hooded vagabond, wields blood-red on a sickle:
A reaper not as grim as death, or fate, but just as fickle.

Roman Fountain

The groping bodies meld atop a comber
Raised by hands and molds of sculptural Rome.
Rome the Colossus. The Very Much that births
The More. Flesh-colored cloudlets like trompe l'oeil
Dangle above the piazza's winking eye.

Brickwork at the nearby bathhouse ruin
Swells then shimmers inward, set in motion
By the hot glare of frolicking bronze nudes
Splashing in endless — one might say eternal —
Foreplay. Their hands are clasping metal manes

Of mares and stallions launched from pools of bracing
Spring water, which traveled downhill all this way
To gush the moments into marble bowls,
Over whose rims the water all the while . . .
. . . How to say it? breaks its crystal smile?

Which, by the way, is what the nymphs are doing.
They don't have to sublimate, being
The sublimation. It is a proper orgy,
Fin de siècle style, in the name of Art.
Each bimbo naiad has a Rambo triton,

Exerting quads and biceps to arise
From the terrific nether-pull of bronze,
The humdrum roundabouts of cars and scooters,
The crazed inertia of the modern city.
Rome that defies you: *Go ahead and eat me!*

The stomachs of the epochs and the mouths
Of popes and emperors ratified this truth.
Who gave bronze and stone such appetites?
Rome eats itself in saucy *bocconcini*,
And when it's done it licks its fingers clean.

Out and Back in Rome

PERIPHERY

A sphere compressed with refuse rolls through the city.
The *urbs* is like a tumbleweed blowing
Across this ghost town in the commonwealth
Of garbage. I have no idea where I am going
When I get lost in Rome's periphery.
Whatever's left of me I keep by stealth.

RETURN

The pastel pink and peach *palazzi*
Have cornices that slash the sky.
A dreadlocked woman with a pack
Of mutts under the Ponte Marconi
Reins her hellhounds in on leashes.
They snap at me like something meaty,
Growling, *Let's rip him, shred by shred!*
When the woman hollers, *Scemi! Zitti!*
Her dreadlocks snake around her head.

TRANSIT

My arms are swaying while I stand,
Bowing my head as the bus ride
Jolts my body side to side.

We passengers are urban trees.
Resolutely reaching, our hands
Are sprouting from deciduous sleeves.

If Rome is fun, in sun it's even more so,
And I just bought some wingtips on the Corso
To glide along where couples smooch and play,
And hear a woman with her lover say
His yellow tie is *molto elegante.*
The sapphire sky, like angel's breath in Dante,
Absolves us from resolve, while mannequins
In decked *vetrine* envy us our skins.
A migrant peddler pesters me to barter,
His raw hand proffering some cheesy loot he
Gets his meals with. O Saint Agnes, martyr,
Many are the ways of dying into beauty.

Afterlife in the Provinces

In Orvieto, the punishing dullness of life
Rehashes a dualist drama, as the dreariness
Of its cliffs rehearses in January. All earth,
The fire that made them has long since frozen
To resignation in tufa, grizzled as the eyes
Of *negozianti*, unsublimable despite the Duomo.

The only inhabitant that surmounts it is the Duomo,
Which, while you're just getting on with your life,
Pops up with a loud *ta-da!* catching your eye
Like the ineradicable blotches and stains of dreariness
It rises above. A primeval volcano's frozen
Upchuck deposited a citadel of earth,

Which the Orvietani, pretenders to Etruscan earth,
Made a one-way proposition topped by a Duomo.
Walk the Corso in midwinter when the frozen
Pedestrians in furs prompt you to wonder how life
Has persisted so long, despite the dreariness
Of parading it daily for the same people's eyes.

To Henry James's uppity Grand Tour eyes,
From the moment he alighted on the face of the earth
At the foot of the *rupe*, Orvieto's dreariness
Seemed but the slag heap of the smelting Duomo,
Whose Technicolor facade winks to an afterlife
James will believe in when (if then) hell is frozen.

Is it merely the monotony in which custom has frozen,
A habitual crossing of *t*'s and dotting of *i*'s,
That has long since knocked the *f* out of life?
Is it row upon row of palazzos the color of earth
On the strangling backstreets that lead to the Duomo,
Hideouts for microbes and the mildew of dreariness?

It's hard to identify the sources of dreariness
When you've become part of a routine so frozen
You share *pettegolezzi* in Piazza del Duomo
On Sundays, or prop up the background for travelers' eyes
Rummaging images, a citizen of the Village Earth
Atop a medieval bump in modern life.

Even if life-in-death does away with dreariness,
Your body is earth, into which has frozen
Your eyes' light, which shines in the spires of the Duomo.

Baba Yaga and the Midsummer Night

"Why a little curtain of flesh on the bed of our desire?"
William Blake

A clear midsummer night with wisps
Of dreamy distance looms above
The vacancy and for-sale signs.

The crabgrass has grown high, scratchy
As anxious wishes, while insects love
The seeded parts of empty lots.

My house my house my house,
My chicken-claw skull-bone house.

In the beginning was the image,
Then the flesh, then the creation
Of what could not escape or stay.

But where the light was, all was different,
Fine, clear, and granted: the baby
Gazing up at eyes gazing down.

You find you're drawn to the odd
Swivel-house of God.

A hot air current plods the land.
Space soars high, a big sprawling torsion
Of cricket song, the black milk spilled,

And the heart drenched in unseeing.
The many-in-one are reaching out
To clasp their hidden healing portion.

Just feel how my touch lingers
While I sample your fingers.

In town on Main Street people primp
And preen, their wishes grazing skin,
And then the show it's no big deal,

But touch me and it's all over,
Touch my bod, I'll bust my fetters
And cover you in light-as-feathers.

It's a question of who gets dibs
When my stick rakes your ribs.

Prayer at the Winter Solstice

2017

God of flu and laryngitis,
God of via negativas
Iced on roads and anti-Midas
Touches of our fallen divas:

God of cracks along the walk,
Cracked republics, and of kitsch,
God of failure's watch in hock,
God of the raw sexual itch:

God of wrists in morgues, just dead,
God the breaking wave suspends
Over hearts that lose their head,
Ray of light the water bends:

God of flies whose buzzing fills
Emptiness's dazzling quiddity,
God of the worst of all our ills,
Insurmountable stupidity:

Thwart our knowing what we're praying
Till the sun at night is clearer,
Let the blindness we're betraying
See the twilight in your mirror.

Trump l'Oeil

Switching the spotlight on with brand-new coins,
We craned our necks. Now, though we try and try,
We can't make out the ceiling: only sky
Where Puttis' chubby thighs recede to loins.
What art! Where granite architecture joins
With plaster, the light-and-dark our naked eye
Can't see as brushstrokes tells a beautiful lie.
Columns converge in vaulted, yielding groins.

Up there, foreshortening prolongs the height
Indefinitely. Birds are tweeting round
The Patron's head, gold-plated clouds enthrone
The Militant Elect, and a skull bone
With wings suggests that even Death's unbound.
It seems to climb forever, but not quite.

You pilgrims walking by, oblivious

You pilgrims walking by, oblivious,
Your minds, it seems, on something not at hand,
Can you have come from such a distant land
(The way you look suggests as much to us)
That you're not weeping, even as you pass
Right through the suffering city, like that band
Of people who, it seems, don't understand
A thing about the measure of its loss?

If you would only stop so you could hear
About it all (so says my sighing heart),
Your eyes would fill with tears before you leave.
For she who blessed the city is nowhere
In sight: what words about her we impart
Have force enough to make a stranger grieve.

The Country of Fire

All that isn't burnt won't live here.
All that isn't a granule of earth,
Wrapped inside a nascent word,
Parches into pieces and breaks away.
Severe and impartial, the drought
Broods on the reservoir.

Look into mother's mirror:
Your beloved face is a nest
Of dried-up mud and twigs
The swallows long ago abandoned,
Your eyes open wide a gorge
In which animals find no water.

The calm of night is withered,
The same air hangs in every
Sigh. There is no beginning,
No end, in the country of fire.
Your every wish returns to cling
To a rack of bones, and burns.

A Short History of War on TV

Old newsreels of world wars
Are all in black and white.
Demagogues at podiums gesture
To swells in a sea of people
Wavy with handkerchief whitecaps,
And soldiers with guns and cigarettes
Seem confident their girls are waiting
In a flurry of winking confetti.

Later we see the camouflage
Background trying to surface.
The rice paddies look pastel,
And the soldiers blanch, fatigued.
Peasants the color of straw
Run from burning straw huts,
And the roof of the pallid jungle
Grows rank in our televisions.

Then grains of sand replace
The grainy image. An oasis
Shimmers on the evening news
But is gone when the army reaches it.
Flames in bombarded buildings
Undulate like indolent djinns,
And the city looks eerily vacant,
Its inhabitants scattered afar.

The lens angle widens, encompassing
A front that has got our backs.
A car careens into a crowd
Of news-camera women and men
Fleeing a story they beam
Into screens of our own devices,
Like clips of the film called *World*
That fits in our palms as we run.

Out of the thick clouds' core

Out of the thick clouds' core,
Down — burnished, the cuirass's
Dazzling yellow zigzag course,
With bursting sound, a rushing roar —
Plummets the whirlwind and dashes
On currents ridden headlong like a horse
Over farmland and homes, and wages war;
But when it crashes into a city,
Its links of mail hinged no more,
It darkens like rings under eyes,
And zigzag and sound and wind
Become anxiety
Of tortured busyness confined:
And without a fight it slays.

An Old Italian Watching the News

He got his tight lip in the orphanage
When he was small. Doing what he was told,
He learned that even children can be old,
And soon became a man of every age.

He's watching television's daily scene
Of neighborhoods in battle zones, blown up.
It makes him weep to be an old grown-up
Watching the people weeping on the screen.

His grief's not simply for the families' dead,
Or humankind, or superhuman force.
His face becomes a grimace of remorse —
A moment only, then he drops his head,

As though he's trying to remember how,
Not that he feels regret for his delaying
What is now past and well beyond his saying.
Neglecting what he never knew, he now

Can know some pieces of what isn't gone.
The people with their faces in their hands
For him recall both war and reprimands.
He has become a father weeping for his son.

Pilgrim

He started out a favored son of Florence,
Most bellicose among Love's devotees.
An arrow early barbed his boyish ease.
The mythic monsters of his own abhorrence
And love swallowed him, spat him out. Adherents
Of papal power and the fleur-de-lis
Seized all except a sieve of memories
He'd use to strain existence from appearance.

Exile was his stability: the salt
Of others' bread, his beggar's role, the cares
He cauterized and bandaged phrase by phrase.
In lieu of pilgrimage he spent his days
Ascending and descending others' stairs,
As if in restless search of grace in fault.

Retired from Hell, Paolo Says It Was Heaven

INFERNO V

Aroused beside her, I went mute
Because my every word was pinned
To shredded semaphores of wind,
And my resistance now was moot.
Her gentleness put on a storm.
Beauty without a stitch of cloth's
A bonfire crackling with moths.
I rose and tumbled with her form.

She flared. Maybe I seemed depraved
To those who watch the sun's eclipse
Through a glass, darkly, but I caved
In, helpless, when she twitched her hips.
Our favored region was the nether
As we held tight against the weather.

The Ideal

You can't not take him anywhere:
    His mimicry's sublime,
And he is knocking at your door
    Eternally on time.

His suit is white, his hair is black,
    As yours was recently.
He is your younger look-alike,
    Your on-demand esprit.

He's heading to the party now,
    But you don't want to go,
Since unlike him you don't know how
    To say what's apropos.

He sits with you while you relax
    With wine or chamomile.
You laud and envy that he lacks
    The shyness you revile.

Is there a chance you'd take my place?
    You timidly begin.
He says: *I'll be your carapace,*
    Your nothingness within.

Etruscan Tomb: An Inventory

VILLA GIULIA, ROME

One hand mirror, two amphoras,
Three amphoras, four;

Five figured vases
Arranged around the door;

Six miniature warriors
Recalling heroic lore;

Seven little, eight little warriors,
In bronze, without the gore;

Nine painted musicians
Playing a silent encore;

Ten partying patricians;
And happily, a whore.

A Contemplative Considers Show Biz

Maybe I'll start a chorus line
Of mystics: gaunt with God and diet,
They'll time their cancan kicks at Quiet
After a Moulin Rouge design.
Their whirling will be all the rage:
Swinging their swanky skirts and shoes,
Directed by Juan de la Cruz,
To big-band music of the spheres.
I want my troupe to take the stage
Like a flash inside a cloud.
Solitude will be a crowd
And Silence let out raucous cheers
And Emptiness get in for free,
Attracted by the bright marquee.

On the Cutting Down of a Pine Tree

The pine tree has been chopped outside the window
That frames the backdrop to my armchair life.
A Christmas tree a neighbor planted years
Ago, it grew — gangly, inelegant — above
The balcony and roof, its upper branches
Lacking an angel, but alive with doves
In pairs that used to pass their summers there.

Once a gathering place for gifts and carols,
In its dotage the tree became a gnarly realist,
Impassive to traffic, rigid and imbalanced
As a man who can't recall when he last danced.

The town decided all such trees are perils
To plain priorities of cars and wires.
But local finches loved its shade and seed,
And its scaly bark and scrawny branches oddly
Fit in, like a grubby, kindly corner store.
I'm looking toward what's missing now, aware
My gaze has gone off giddy in the air,
Leaving me here to make friends with my words.

The whistling in my head is memory's birds.

Song of Achille, the Bottle Man

When he was young he had his pride,
And thought his pride would never end,
But now his dearest friends have died
And he has no country to defend,
He hobbles out a daily beat
While gathering bottles from the street.

Sometimes he puts a good drunk on,
And folds at playing cards too late
To win the day. His money's gone
When he reels home to wife and fate,
And in the windows' darkened maws
Glimpses what his father was.

He'll slip a bit on rotten fruit
On cobbles, shouting something base
At shadows. He can be a brute
To Giulia too. She slaps his face,
But then makes room for him in bed
When he crawls in, the rest unsaid.

He dreams night is an empty bottle
With other bottles in a stall,
The lot of them as dumb as cattle
Asleep beneath a silent pall,
All left there when he left off work,
Their empty bodies full of dark.

The Fever

In a shuttered room, a boy
Hears the nearby breathing sea.
His mother towels his brow
And sings rhymes from the nursery.

Jack, oh Jack be nimble,
Stick your thumb in a festive pie.
You're in a corner, Jack,
Don't fade away now, quick, come back!

He stares, the room withers.
Its walls curl, the wainscot blisters.
A golden bowl of sunlight
Brims the table late at night.

Your life's in a thimble, low
And trembling, while a candlestick
Awaits your leap. Now pick:
Eeny meeny miny moe!

Her gentle voice fluoresces
Through his veins. In her body's translucence,
He sees a doubloon-moon
Aglow in the brackish bones of a schooner.

Winter Solstice

The world is a book with its pages torn out.
Walk along the sidewalk — you'll find some tonight,
Crumpled, perhaps, or pasted to the asphalt —

Or skittering at your feet, copies of copies,
Dropped by obsolete amanuenses,
Their palsied hands saluting infirmity . . .

A page is different when you turn it:
Just as day was, when night, the picture-book,
Emptied its frames, and snowfall came,
And made all the pages blank and perfect.

III

THE POETRY OF ABSENCE

I am what is not what it was.

KATHLEEN RAINE

Paradiso XX.1–30

When he who lights up all the world descends
So low that, in our hemisphere, the white
Of day wears thin and bit by bit day ends,

The heavens, which only he till now made bright,
Appear all of a sudden to the eye:
Numerous sparkles of a single light.

I called to mind those gestures of the sky
When the ensign of the world and heads of state
That formed its sacred beak left off its cry,

Because those living lights poured forth a spate
Of brilliance when they sang — fugitive sound
My memory cannot grasp or re-create.

O love whose loveliness is wrapped around
With joy, those melodies your breath inspires
Were flute-notes blown by thought that grace had found!

When all those incandescent, prized sapphires
Studded across the sixth celestial sphere
Had hushed their resonant angelic choirs,

It seemed a river's purl was drawing near,
Tripping along downhill from stone to stone —
The bounty of its mountain source made clear;

The way, along a soundboard, hums the tone
Of a guitar, or from a hullabaloo
Of bagpipes breath propels a steady drone,

Just so, without delay or more ado,
The Eagle's purling rose up in its throat
As if its body were an open flue.

There it took voice, and then came out a note
Formed by its beak into the shape of words
I waited for — my heart is where I wrote.

Logos

The form the branches take is who I am,
As is the trunk in seed whose cue I am.

Blowflies hatching in a corpse display,
Perpetually, how impromptu I am.

What's dying, being born? Who's mothering
The names of things, ancient and new? I am.

Many have drawn my water, but no well
Contains the single drop of dew I am.

The seasons make their odyssey around
The vacant pinpoint sky of blue I am.

No source of light on earth illuminates
The place a rainbow ends, the hue I am.

Let there be light is what I call myself,
And being dark is what I do. I am

The thought you have of me, the fire of love
Consuming what you thought you knew I am.

The Archer and the target that he hit,
The arrow that he fit *and drew*, I am.

Francis and the Weaver

ISOLA MAGGIORE, LAKE TRASIMENO,

LENT CA. 1210

One day, when yellow crucifer was in flower,
The gravel lurch of a boat disturbed the shore.
A girl was out to watch the waves a while
Before she sat down at her loom to toil.
She hid herself nearby: the man looked rough,
His shepherd's smock in tatters. He beached his skiff,
Slung his pack on his shoulder, and trudged upslope.
She prayed her rosary as she walked home.
Later, that day of ashes, she thought of the stranger.
Grimy, he'd seemed like a barely smothered cinder,
Or the soot part of a wick, the part that reddens.
His legs and arms were strong, his expression hidden.

During the forty days, sometimes they met
When he'd come downhill carrying the dust
That haloed him. Her father paid a debt
Of bread for work, and he'd leave. He never fussed
Or asked for more, too gentle to pose a threat.
She felt a pull whenever she caught his eye,
Like falling upward in a starry sky.

They let him be, demented up in the copse,
Where scattered branches were the drifter's fuel.
They figured that voices were taking up his talk.
The ash of him by day; at night, a small,

Red flame that pierced the hilltop like a flickering
Flower. From her window she'd see it leaping,
And ponder what kept a man outdoors that long
And in that season. Her father, uncles, siblings
Were silent too while there were chores still left
To do, tending the crops until they sat
Together inside a gauzy circle of light.

She'd sit and weave her cloth like light in the weft
Of darkness where their island home was spread.
She could inhabit the silence of her kindred:
A cottage with walls, a hearth, and doors that fasten.
The stranger's seemed like woods where she'd get lost.
Or Trasimeno when the sky turns ashen,
And buckles with heavy clouds that touch the hills,
The lake aroused like flesh in a sudden gust.

Rosemary

It's a bush
        beside a barricade
That keeps kids
        from kicking their ball
Into the startled street
        of streaming cars.
It's a heady green
        hidden in dusk-hue,
Its sheen shaded
        like a pale shell,
The lining of which
        is liminal pearl.
The gas meter
        measures our methane
Consumption in units
        of use, yes,
But what's cooked wallows
        (even in winter)
In a sprig my fingers
        spring and splinter
When Daphne is working
        that day's dinner
Into broth. The branch
        transforms what it brushes.
Like a post-flood dove
        who proffers peace,

Tweezing a twig

                 between my beaky

Thumb and finger,

                    I fritter a fragrance

Like sea-dew

            of a distant deluge.

To the Sun in March

AFTER TOMMASO CAMPANELLA

The murdered mud was what was left of ground
When winter stuck a dagger in the air
And the sky lay in a culvert, gagged and bound.

Now, azure's eye and mind's hello, you're here.
Your heat is calling all the mothers home.
Cadavers toss their mummy cloths and stare.

Small lizards creep from under the loosened hedgerow,
Getting news from last year's tongues of leaves.
The earthworms thread the corridors of loam.

Why, then, with motions filling rooted lives,
And all this coming round, am I ungreen,
My heart a hardened husk no sprout relieves?

You spring of light and seeping dawn, turbine
Of heaven, the one star here that isn't cold:
Ignite my senses, pierce my sight unseen.

This fringe of skin's the fiber of the world.
I'll be a kernel, cracked, that dilates light,
A germ who's in a nation made of curled
Beginnings, when you penetrate my night.

Maya in Two Movements

DAYLIGHT

Each ray of light is speaking fluent sun.
The asphalt's skin secretes the oil of noon
And packed crust dusts my shoes. The air dries vapor
On my face, whose aspects mime the moon
Like ghostly watermarks on pallid paper.

I am an acolyte of light that brings
Me to the brink of dark, where sunlight hangs
Precariously balanced, or I'm benighted.
At dawn the first bird sings, the way that things
Which always are have always been requited.

TWILIGHT

A woman in a yellow dress
Seated on a fountain's edge
Outside a station at dusk, her face
Imbued in passing with the body's
Dream of perpetuity in rest.

Phenomena

I mistook that hummingbird
For a dragonfly at first,
Metallic green
Stopping and starting
Beside the porch
Then zoning in on bushes
And birdbath fast,
As life is so short
As not to outlast
The falling of an apple.
Make up your mind, Andrew,
Pray or fall asleep.
But pray to whom?
Petition the warm green light,
My lips are blades
Of grass to praise the wind.
Nothing else to do really
But get buzzing and dream,
Ache in the finger joints
And shine like dull metal.

Trying to Remember the Myth of Poppies

TERMINI STATION, ROME

Anemones have theirs, and ancient women
Would beat their breasts for that delicious red,
But I don't know what story makes these human
Or joins their dribbled brilliance with the dead.
The jolt of color must have roused a tale
From someone once. Vermilion in crabgrass,
Gravel, and glass, their petals' flesh is frail
As reckless adolescents trembling en masse.

I gaze a bit before I leave the train,
Searching for words that perished on my tongue
Too soon to hear. I rummage through my brain
For what's still left of that unsettling song.
There no doubt was a person in the past
Who gave his breath to them and spoke, aghast.

And: A Spring Forecast

If things fly off in every no-direction
And you can't tell the fullness from the frayed,
And waves are freighted on the lake with shade,
And you keep tripping on your own erection,

And your hair's mussed up and what you leave unfinished
Is everything you start, and there won't be
A lake for you in winter's memory,
And surplus is what's left when dearth's diminished,

And mild temperatures give way to freeze,
And innocence is lust and love is lost,
And good-to-go is ever tempest-tossed
Without a sextant or a judge to please,

And Sunday walkers stop to watch the waders
From the shore as if to prove a promise
Jesus never made to doubting Thomas,
And moms with carriages are rollerbladers

With babies smiling at the face they're in,
And worry's eating you and you eat fish,
And even all the world is half your wish,
And Sun the busker always beats his tin,

And here and now will never be repeated,
And all the happy dogs who splash in waves
Are Saint Bernards a sense of purpose saves,
And you most want and fear to be defeated,

Decisively, within the hub of zero
Spiders weave beside the cyclers' path,
And dulcet harmonies of songbird wrath
Are soundtracks for your paint-by-numbers hero,

And the earth is slow and unafraid of dark,
Patient with tangled roots and full of pity
For how the naked moment makes you giddy:
Then knock is open wide, and luck's a lark.

Guido, I think it would be great if you

Guido, I think it would be great if you,
Lapo, and I were seized by magic, placed
Together in a little boat that raced
The breeze to go where we all wanted to;
So neither storm nor throes of fate could do
A thing to interrupt our steady-paced
Advance, and all of us had so embraced
One goal, that our affection always grew.

And Lapo's Lucy and your Vanna now,
Along of course with she whose beauty blows
Away the thirty best, appear somehow;
And we discuss — guess what? (it starts with *L*).
And they would be delighted with us beaus,
And I believe that we'd be pleased as well.

From the tautened image

From the tautened image
I keep the moment's vigil
With imminence of waiting,
And I expect no one:
In shadow that is lit
I eye the doorbell,
Which imperceptibly emits
A pollen-cloud of sound —
And I expect no one:
Between four walls
Astonished by space
Greater than a desert
I expect no one.
But he must come,
Will come, if I resist
And bloom unnoticed,
Come of a sudden,
When I expect it least;
Will come like pardon
For what brings death,
Will come to make me sure
Of his and my treasure,
Will come like solace
For my own sorrows and his,
Will come, perhaps already comes,
His whisper.

Non-Noah and the Rainbow

Each day I need a refresher course
In living, something, a prayer maybe,
Condensing in the air of me.

I rise, open the blinds half-mast,
Fold up the night, unfold the news:
All shapes of light I can't refuse.

I'm shadow in the midst, at most
Non-Noah, arkless in the flood
Of absence that's my element.

Not completely though. Some shred
That I don't know is a tensile thread
In the blue, a rainbow filament.

After the storm I walk in mud
And look up at the motley crest
The disappearing moisture leaves,

And birds conveying branches from land
And the bow is bent to the Dyer's hand
And the eye is transparent that perceives.

Waves

SURF

The ever-moving never-changing face
Spreads and retracts, away from going back.
Waves are awareness, and horizons' sphere
Contains them in a perfect now and here.
The inlet on the shore of what they lack
Becomes the spindle of their broken lace.

BREAKERS

The soft departure of the tattered waves
Leaves luster on the sand like empty graves.

RIPPLES

Enter
Mild crystalline
Puckering crosshatched gently
Rocking blue-green eyeball to see
Stillness.

WHITECAPS

Looking out to sea,
What matter, poetry?
Poems are words on waves
That only drowning saves.

May Day Black Locust

The longer I look
At the dry brown pods
And white, bell-shaped,
Honey-fragrant blossoms
Among which the bees
Are plunging their heads,
The more the bees seem
The moving members
Of the tree's flourish,
As the stream nearby
Is its running commentary,
And I, the observer,
Am taking notes on myself.

August

Beside the lapped pier,
In time with heat, cicadas
Percuss and rasp their brass.
A dinghy, like a carcass
Discarded, bobs in glare.

Refracted in blackwater,
We've come down to the fringe
Of foam, where dragonfly eggs
In strings and nymph-stage
Carapaces undulate.

The sunlight rolls on its side
As the day squints down at murk,
Returning to the circling
Clasp of summer succulence,
The long-armed queen of weeds.

Anamnesia

A silvering mirror is the deepest of wells.
Finding yourself in an other, you say,
"How did you get there and where was the way
We divided, becoming somebody else?"

Home is a starting point. Exile is origin.
The self is passed between hands like a bead,
Inspected in loupes and forgot in a bin;
Disappears for years and comes back black seed.

As a kid walking home from school you had it,
A bovine oblivious to birds on its back.
You traipsed in a stretch of afternoon shadow,
Lost in distraction and your family's lack.

Your wondering blood used to stream in your thought,
But now, the past dead, you've turned to the earth,
When, out of a blur, the star of your birth
Reflects in the depths of a face you forgot.

Aeolian

The wind had words for me that day,
Though what it said I couldn't say
Or argue with when it arose
Across a land where nothing grows
And billowed in my open mouth.
I hadn't known there was a drought
Or ever thought of breath as deference,
When all at once wind made the difference,
Filling the space of where I was
As if I'd sighed without a cause.
Whatever mind wind might forebode
Deciphered its remorseless code
Prior to wind and mind's conjunction,
Which I forgot without compunction.

Dialectic

Parmenides said the world's abstract.
Democritus claimed that space is packed.
Plato spanned the universe.
Aristotle's prose was terse.
Copernicus found that other spheres
Than Ptolemy's were in arrears.
Descartes, Locke, Hume, and Kant
Met with God to talk detente.
Berkeley's stone did not exist.
Johnson kicked it and shook his fist.
Einstein knocked down Newton's blocks.
The nursery sued and changed its locks.
With Crick and Watson's spiral key
The landlord, man, is absentee.

The Poetry of Absence

FOR A WIDOWED FRIEND

"Love makes us one with the very object of these words."
St.-John Perse

To make a thing, first *be* the thing
Before the deed of making was:
His hands and eyes fashion a ring
That's shaped by shaping its own cause.

His heart conceives a will beyond
Its circumstance, while love in act
Creates from nil as if a wand
Spilled ink across the barest fact,

And ink spelled breath's arithmetic.
The widower-poet doesn't think,
In waiting for the grace or trick
To still the waves where ashes sink.

He speaks the brightness of the dark.
His heart already out at sea,
The angel-pilot guides the barque
Of souls to where his words would be.

The Harvest and the Lamp

It's not the things the earth contains,
Buried riches and burrowed shames,
Heating up the deeper they rest
While diamonds form beneath the crust.

It's not the hedges' evening meld,
Nor is it the harvest field
Nestled in the mothering hills
And sounding vesper's seeded bells.

It's not the daydream of the girl
Working a birch to leave her scrawl
Of names and shapes of love or hate
The bark will suture in its cut.

It's not the ministry of crows
On branching pulpits preaching news
About the lanes that lead to doors
The dead have passed through unawares.

And considering the skyey circuits,
Streaked with the damp of departed spirits,
It's not the shadows the planets cast
While star fields prostrate toward the west.

It's not. It's always where they were,
Like a fire still burning in an empty camp.
We leave the door of the dark ajar,
For things in their lives are the eye of the lamp.

NOTES

A CASALINGA IN SPRING

casalinga: housewife
marmo finto: fake marble, imitation marble flooring
Maremmano: a bull bred on the Maremma, a region on the west coast
   of Tuscany

ROMAN FOUNTAIN

bocconcini: nibbles or small bites

OUT AND BACK IN ROME

urbs: Latin for "city," specifically Rome
palazzi: apartment buildings
Scemi! Zitti!: "Idiots! Shut up!"
Corso: the Via del Corso, a main street in central Rome
molto elegante: very elegant
vetrine: shop display windows

AFTERLIFE IN THE PROVINCES

negozianti: shopkeepers   *rupe*: cliff
Duomo: cathedral   *pettegolezzi*: gossip
Corso: Main Street

BABA YAGA AND THE MIDSUMMER NIGHT

In Russian fairytales, the witch or supernatural being Baba Yaga dwells
in a forest and lives in a hut that stands on chicken legs and is partially
made of human bones.

DANTE: YOU PILGRIMS WALKING BY, OBLIVIOUS

Dante places this sonnet in the penultimate episode of his prosimetrum
the *Vita nova*, where not long after Beatrice's death he see pilgrims pass-
ing through Florence on the way to Rome. "She who blessed the city"
translates lowercase *beatrice*, which means "she who blesses."

CLEMENTE REBORA: OUT OF THE CLOUDS' THICK CORE

Clemente Rebora (1885–1957), a leading early Italian modernist poet, was from Milan. *Dall'intensa nuvolaglia* is from his first collection, *Frammenti lirici* (1913). In 1936, Rebora became a Catholic priest in the Rosminian order and wrote almost exclusively religious-doctrinal poetry from then on.

DANTE: PARADISO XX.1–30

In this scene, Dante and Beatrice are in the sphere of Jupiter, the sixth stage of their ascent to the Empyrean. Dante's interlocutor is the imperial eagle — the shape of a heraldic eagle made up of the individual lights of monarchs and other leaders who represent Justice. The last canto ended with a denunciation of leaders in Christendom who were *not* just; "left off its cry," in line 9, refers to that speech at the end of canto XIX. At the end of this passage, Dante wants to know the names of the spirits in this heaven, which he will then inscribe in his heart.

ROSEMARY

rosemary: from the Latin *ros marinus*, "sea dew"

DANTE: GUIDO, I THINK IT WOULD BE GREAT IF YOU

Guido Cavalcanti (1255–1300) was an influential Florentine lyric poet and a close friend of Dante in their youth. Lapo Gianni (died after 1328) was a poet in the group of poets around Dante and Guido Cavalcanti, known to us as the *stilnovisti*, or poets who wrote in the "sweet new style." The women mentioned in the poem were the main female protagonists of their love poetry.

CLEMENTE REBORA: FROM THE TAUTENED IMAGE

Rebora composed *Dall'immagine tesa* in 1920.

ACKNOWLEDGMENTS

I am grateful to the editors of the following online and print publications in which these poems first appeared, sometimes in earlier versions: *Able Muse, Alabama Literary Review, America, Angle, Blue Unicorn, Chimaera, Christianity and Literature, Comstock Review, Dante Today, Dappled Things, First Things, Hudson Review, Kenyon Review, Light, Literary Imagination, Lucid Rhythms, Measure, Modern Age, New Criterion, New Formalist, Orbis, Orchards, Poetry Daily, Presence, Sacred Web, Southwest Review, Temenos Academy Review, Think, Unsplendid, Valparaiso Poetry Review, Verse Daily.* Some of the poems were previously collected, in earlier versions, in my chapbook *Death of a Dissembler* (White Violet Press, 2014); my thanks to Karen Kelsay for permission to reprint them.

I also gratefully acknowledge Edizioni Rosminiane Sosalitas s.a.s. (Stresa, Italy) for permission to publish my translations from Clemente Rebora, and Northwestern University Press for permission to reprint (with minor emendations) my translation from Dante, *You pilgrims walking by, oblivious*, which originally appeared in my translation of the *Vita nova* (Evanston, Illinois, 2012).

I am indebted to poets at Eratosphere for feedback on many of the poems in this collection.

My thanks to James Matthew Wilson for his editorial conscientiousness and insight. And thanks also to Sarah Wear for directing this book into and through production.

I am grateful to Gaynor Goffe for doing the calligraphy that appears on the cover and title pages.

As always, my profoundest debt is to my wife, Daphne. This book is dedicated to her.